21 Day Devotional
Declaration of Faith

21 Day Devotional Declaration of Faith

James Raphael
Foreword by Bishop Donald Hilliard, Jr., D. Min.

Copyright 2017 James Raphael
Published by James Raphael Enterprises (JRE)
Freehold, NJ
JamesRaphaelEnterprises@gmail.com
www.jamesraphael.com
ISBN-13: 9780692852200
ISBN-10: 0692852204
All rights reserved.
Library of Congress Control Number: 2017955935
James Raphael Enterprises (JRE)

Scripture quotations are taken from the New King James Version® (NKJV). Copyright © 1982 by Thomas Nelson. Used by permission. All rights reserved.

Scripture quotations are taken from King James Version (KJV)
Public Domain

Scripture quotations are taken from *Holy Bible*, New Living Translation (NLT) copyright © 1996, 2004, 2015 by Tyndale House Foundation. Used by permission of Tyndale House Publishers Inc., Carol Stream, Illinois 60188. All rights reserved.

Scripture quotations are taken from Holy Bible, New International Version®, NIV® Copyright ©1973, 1978, 1984, 2011 by Biblica, Inc.® Used by permission. All rights reserved worldwide.

Scripture quotations are taken from New American Standard Bible (NASB) Copyright © 1960, 1962, 1963, 1968, 1971, 1972, 1973, 1975, 1977, 1995 by The Lockman Foundation

I dedicate this book to my wife, Dr. Monaé Raphael, and our son, James Du Bois Raphael. I have learned so much being a husband and a dad. I look forward to increasing my wisdom, knowledge, and understanding to impact my family, the kingdom of God, and the world positively. Monaé, I thank you for your support and sacrifice. With your support, I can reach my goals and fulfill my God-given purpose. You are truly a trooper. I appreciate you, I thank you, and I love you!

To all who would like to nurture a deeper spiritual relationship with God, and reflect on His word for strength, direction, and continuous faith, this book is for you. I say that your spiritual walk with God is a journey and not a destination.

To all who have something to say about the goodness of God but are afraid to say it and express it, this book is for you. I pray that you find the courage to allow God to speak to you and through you to reach unbelievers and to edify the body of Christ.

To all leaders and aspiring leaders, this book is for you. I encourage you to continue to learn and develop yourselves to strengthen others to become their best.

To all those who have more questions than answers, this book is for you. I ask that you be patient and systematically search God's word for answers. I encourage you to continue to believe that God can answer your questions and guide you to reach your highest potential in all aspects of your life.

Acknowledgments

Lord, I thank you for saving me and making me your son. Thank you for giving me favor, courage, and the desire to reach my destiny.

Special thanks to my wife for her prayers, and ideas during our brainstorming sessions.

Thanks to my son, James Du Bois Raphael. At the age of two, you have taught me the meaning of unwavering love. Seeing your progress, as a child with autism, means the world to me. We believe God for our miracle. I love you, son!

Thanks to my mom, Vadnie Marius; my dad, Beauvais Raphael; my stepmother, Elmase; and my extended family for their prayers and their words of encouragement during this process.

Thanks to Bishop Donald Hilliard, Jr., my pastor; Dr. Odessa McNeill; Dr. Joanne Noel; Joseph Duffy and Deacon Thomas Lukoma for reading the *21 Day Devotional: Declaration of Faith* manuscript. Thanks to Cathedral International leaders and the congregation for their prayers and support.

Thanks to my in-laws, Bishop Marcus A. Johnson, Sr. and Evangelist Ronaé A. Johnson, for their prayers and support. Thanks to the leaders of New Harvest Ministries, Inc. and the congregation for their prayers and support.

Contents

Foreword · xi
Introduction · xiii

Day 1   God's Protection · 1
Day 2   God's Companionship · 7
Day 3   God's Love · 13
Day 4   God's Presence · 19
Day 5   Don't Quit · 25
Day 6   God's Knowledge and Purpose · · · · · · · · · · · · · · · · · · 31
Day 7   Shield of Faith · 37
Day 8   Distractions · 43
Day 9   Pregnancy and Anticipation · 49
Day 10   Focus on God · 55
Day 11   Vision · 61
Day 12   Full Circle · 67
Day 13   The Church · 73
Day 14   Authority of Scripture · 79
Day 15   The Word of God · 85
Day 16   God's Plans for Your Life · 91
Day 17   Salvation · 97
Day 18   Faith in Action · 103
Day 19   Faith through Works · 109

| Day 20 | Friend of God ································· 115 |
| Day 21 | Jesus ··· 121 |

	About the Author································· 125
	Book Description································ 127
	Promotional Statements ··························· 129

Foreword

I am convinced that years from now, historians are going to mark this as one of the most tumultuous, fear-filled, uncertain times in our nation's history. And literally, in every section of the globe, there seems to be trouble: masses of people are without jobs, their health care is threatened, and so many people are walking wounded. As I say often in my sermons, there are those who literally wake up with bitterness for breakfast, loneliness for lunch, and disaster for dinner. Nevertheless, we who believe can take heart, because God keeps watch over His own.

In his first book, *21 Day Devotional: Declaration of Faith*, James Raphael has given us something to think about, something to chew on, and something to build a foundation on. It's encouraging, it's inspiring, and it's comforting. I commend my son in faith for this step of faith.

In addition to this, he is also successfully serving as a certified leadership success trainer, and I encourage your support thereof. We all need somebody to lean on and someone to help us up the ladder to success. Minister James Raphael is that person. He is upbeat, kind, compassionate, caring, always smiling, always reaching out, texting, and calling to check on others. We support James, and I encourage you all to go get a copy, and let's celebrate this work.

Bishop Donald Hilliard, Jr., D. Min.
Senior Pastor, Cathedral International
Perth Amboy, New Jersey

Introduction

Thank you for purchasing this book. *21 Day Devotional: Declaration of Faith is* designed to help the readers reflect on the awesomeness of God in their lives. I pray this devotional helps the readers start a conversation with their friends, families, and colleagues about who God is and how a person can begin or maintain a covenant relationship with God. When I reflect on my life, I see how God has been good to me. His goodness has been consistent in my life even when I was unborn. My mom had been barren for many years. She asked God for a child. In the seventh year, through God's supernatural intervention and medical technology, I was born in Port-au-Prince, Haiti. Throughout my life's journey, I have seen both the mountaintop (earning my MBA) and the valley (at times... concerned for my elderly mother). Through it all, I have learned that God is still in control. The storms did not come to kill me but to teach me. Therefore, I wrote *21 Day Devotional: Declaration of Faith* as a reminder of who God is and what He is capable of doing.

The structure of the book is deliberate. Each chapter opens with a picture and theme that portrays a message found in the Bible. A Bible verse is provided. The substance of the book is found in the twenty-one devotionals. Each devotional is comprised of two hundred to five hundred words. Each devotional ends with an application in the form of a declaration of faith. At the end of each devotional, there are four reflective statements for readers to consider how to apply the themes and concepts presented in their daily lives. I invite readers to go as deep as possible in thinking about the reflective statements. The scriptures in this book have been a source of inspiration to me throughout my life. It is my prayer that this book stirs each reader's faith to see God as a refuge, strength, and the answer to his or her needs. Enjoy the book!

DAY 1
GOD'S PROTECTION
Ps 91:9-11 (NIV)

 James Raphael Enterprises
Inspiring the Leadership Potential in You

DAY 1

God's Protection

§

<u>Psalm 91:9-11</u> (NIV): "If you say, 'The LORD is my refuge,' and you make the Most High your dwelling, no harm will overtake you, no disaster will come near your tent. For he will command his angels concerning you to guard you in all your ways."

Psalm 91 speaks life to anyone who needs God's protection. And on Wednesday, September 14, 2016, I was that person. On an average day, I leave my home at 5:45 a.m. and make the fifty-mile one-way trip to my job. I have become accustomed to my commute and have found ways to make the time more useful by praying; meditating; listening to the news, music, and audiobooks; and reflecting on my to-do list. Around seven that morning, I was driving on the highway, in the far-right lane, at a pace of about fifty miles per hour. All of a sudden, the car in front of me swerved to the left lane. In a split second, I had to swerve to the left also to avoid a three-foot yellow ladder in the middle of the road and cars on my left. It was so unexpected. The entire ordeal happened so fast. I had no warning that I would need to react so quickly. How could my car only graze the ladder lying in the middle of the road? How could I emerge from this near accident with no injuries? How did my car only have two minor scratches on the passenger-side? This entire situation was beyond my control. I know that it was only by God's protection that I did not have a serious car accident. Psalm 91:11 (NIV) says, "For he will command his angels concerning you to guard you in all your ways." I believe that God's angels protected me from a horrible car accident. This experience has strengthened my belief in God. His protection is manifested not just in the big life-saving moments but also in the little things that we take for granted each day. God commands His protection for you and me. We are valuable in the eyes of God, and He demonstrates how valuable we are to Him by protecting us daily. He protects us even when we don't realize it.

Declaration of Faith

My God. I believe without a doubt, Lord, that you are my God, my shield, my protector, my rock, my source, and much more. I declare supernatural protection over my life and over the lives of my family and friends in the name of Jesus.

Day 1: Reflection
God's Protection

Ps 91:9-11 (NIV): "If you say, 'The LORD is my refuge,' and you make the Most High your dwelling, no harm will overtake you, no disaster will come near your tent. For he will command his angels concerning you to guard you in all your ways."

1. Reflect on the key words in the passage that are most relevant to you.
2. Reflect on a time when God protected you.
3. What are two Bible verses that come to mind after reading this passage?
4. What are your thoughts on this particular passage, and how do you think your thoughts will improve in the future?

NOTES

DAY 2

God's Companionship

§

Joshua 1:9 (NLT): "This is my command: be strong and courageous! Do not be afraid or discouraged. For the LORD your God is with you wherever you go."

When I immigrated from the Caribbean to the States, I was introduced to a new system of living, language, and culture. At the age of 12, my sister and I left my mom and extended family in Haiti to live with my dad and stepmom in Brooklyn, New York. I had so many unanswered questions. At the same time, I was excited to be in "the land of opportunity." In retrospect, Joshua 1:9 encapsulates the assurance that I needed from God during this time of transition. In verse 9, God is reminding Joshua that He is with him at all times which includes times of uncertainty. It is refreshing to know that just as God was with Joshua, He was with me. I was afraid of not having total control of the future. I studied and wanted to have great command of the English language and the American culture. I had to stand up to bullying as a teenager and make conscious decisions to say no to the drugs and violence that so many of my classmates succumbed to. God kept me and strengthened me as a student in Vailsburg Middle School, Central High School, Rutgers University, and as a missionary in Ghana, West Africa. Do you think about your plans and strategies that have not yielded the desired results? God knew beforehand all the things that you would face. He already commanded you to be courageous, and He reminded you that He will be with you wherever you go. This is a command that is everlasting, simply because the one who made the command is everlasting. God is encouraging you to know that He can strengthen you and prepare you for the challenges along the way. You are strengthened when you listen to God's voice and when you read, study, and apply His word. In return, God will equip you for the challenges ahead. Notice Joshua heard God's commands and was strengthened. As a result, "Joshua then commanded the officers of Israel, "Go through the camp and tell the people to get their provisions ready" (Joshua 1:10-11, NLT). God is with you even when you feel afraid, alone, unprepared, and uncertain about the future. God is your trusted companion.

Declaration of Faith

God is with me wherever I go. God commands me to be strong and courageous. I trust God even when I cannot see my way clearly. I believe in the living God. This is my declaration in the name of Jesus!

Day 2: Reflection
God's Companionship

Joshua 1:9 (NLT): "This is my command: be strong and courageous! Do not be afraid or discouraged. For the LORD your God is with you wherever you go."

1. Reflect on the key words in the passage that are most relevant to you.
2. Reflect on your relationship with God. Is it a strong relationship? If not, how can you strengthen your personal relationship with God?
3. What are two Bible verses that come to mind after reading this passage?
4. What are your thoughts on this particular passage, and how do you think your thoughts will improve in the future?

NOTES

DAY 3
GOD'S *Love*

Romans 5:8 (NASB)

DAY 3

God's Love

Romans 5:8 (NASB): "But God demonstrates His own love toward us, in that while we were yet sinners, Christ died for us."

Love has many meanings in our world today. In many cases, human *love* is based on how a person feels, which changes over time. Human *love* may be tied to the benefits gained from a relationship. I know my family and friends love me. The love that I receive from family and friends cannot be compared with the love of God. His love is unconditional, everlasting, reassuring, and sacred. God sent his son Jesus to die for the entire world and pay the debt of sin. Through his death, we have life everlasting. "For the wages of sin is death, but the gift of God is eternal life in Christ Jesus our Lord" (Romans 6:23, NIV). Christ died for humanity to give everyone (past, present, and future) the opportunity to accept Him as Lord and receive His unconditional love. Christ loved us first. Jesus demonstrated His love for us by dying for humanity. What a demonstration of love! How do you demonstrate love? Do you care for the poor, clothe the naked, feed the hungry, or visit those in prison? As a husband and father, I demonstrate love by providing for my family, protecting, understanding, and being present for them. As I continue to meditate on God's word, I'm inspired to become more like Christ and demonstrate his selfless love. I see a progressive transformation in my life. I'm not who I was. I intend to become my best self in the future. God's word teaches us how important humanity is to Him. God loves you, and He is waiting for you to acknowledge His love that surpasses all human understanding.

Declaration of Faith
Christ died for me, and I am thankful. Christ loves me, and I am grateful. Lord, Your demonstration of love through Your action speaks of how much You love humanity. This is my declaration in the name of Jesus.

Day 3: Reflection
God's Love

Romans 5:8 (NASB): "But God demonstrates His own love toward us, in that while we were yet sinners, Christ died for us."

1. Reflect on the key words in the passage that are most relevant to you.
2. Reflect on a time that God has demonstrated His love toward you.
3. What are two Bible verses that come to mind after reading this passage?
4. What are your thoughts on this particular passage, and how do you think your thoughts and behavior will improve in the future?

NOTES

DAY 4

God's Presence

❧

Genesis 3:8-9 (NASB): "They heard the sound of the LORD God walking in the garden in the cool of the day, and the man and his wife hid themselves from the presence of the LORD God among the trees of the garden. Then the LORD God called to the man, and said to him, 'Where are you?'"

I vividly recall playing the popular childhood game hide-and-seek with my siblings, cousins, and friends. At home in Port-au-Prince, as the evening breeze floated through the trees, I would close my eyes and start counting. One. Two. Three. Four. Five. As my count got to ten, the loud noises and footsteps would disappear. When I opened my eyes, no one was there. My siblings, cousins, and friends would do their best to hide or disguise themselves. Most times, I found a good number of them. However, a few of the players were experts, and I couldn't ever locate their hiding places. No matter how hard we try, we cannot hide from God. His presence is everywhere at the same time. Psalm 139:7 (NIV) states, "Where can I go from your Spirit? Where can I flee from your presence?" Regardless of our physical position, socioeconomic status, or emotional condition, God knows where we are. Adam and Eve had disobeyed God and hid themselves out of shame from sin. In the key passage, God asked Adam a gut-wrenching question: "Where are you?" God wasn't waiting for Adam to respond in a surface way, revealing literally where he and Eve were standing in the Garden of Eden. God knows everything, and He knew where they were hiding. But this was a soul-searching question, for His prized possessions had fallen out of fellowship (right relationship with Him). They were missing in action. They were gone. They were out of position, and God felt their absence. This age-old question is relevant today. Consider God is asking, Where are you? Let the intended process of introspection begin. God is asking, what is your thought pattern? Are you showing up where it really counts? Do you spend your time cultivating what really matters? Is your life filled with true meaning? As we repent and humble ourselves before God, He hears us and forgives us. God does not expect perfection. He is perfect. Instead of running and hiding from God, He is asking us to run to Him. Where are you really? Regardless of where you are, God wants you to know that He has had you in mind since the beginning of time. In God's presence, we can find out who we are and where we are. I encourage you to evaluate where you are in all aspects of your life and to make a decision to seek God, impact your family, contribute to your community, and make your time count positively.

Declaration of Faith
Lord, I want to be mindful of where I am spiritually and in every aspect of my life. Help me to have a stronger relationship with you. I believe every aspect of my life will be in alignment with your will. This is my declaration in the name of Jesus.

Day 4: Reflection
God's Presence

Genesis 3:8-9 (NASB): "They heard the sound of the LORD God walking in the garden in the cool of the day, and the man and his wife hid themselves from the presence of the LORD God among the trees of the garden. Then the LORD God called to the man, and said to him, 'Where are you?'"

1. Reflect on the key words in the passage that are most relevant to you.
2. Reflect on a time that you were overwhelmed by God's presence. What does the presence of God mean to you?
3. What are two Bible verses that come to mind after reading this passage?
4. What are your thoughts on this particular passage, and how do you think your thoughts and behavior will improve in the future?

NOTES

DAY 5
DON'T *Quit*

Romans 8:37 (NIV)

DAY 5

Don't Quit

❦

Romans 8:37 (NIV): "No, in all these things we are more than conquerors through [Him] who loved us."

"In all these things" may mean different things to different people. For you, it may mean in the midst of managing your home, family, elderly parents, and your business. For another, it may mean possible transitions with his or her career, ministry, empty nest, or a challenging doctor's report that challenged his or her faith to the core. However, Romans 8:37 states "We are more than conquerors" (NIV). Paul, the writer, acknowledges all the issues, shortcomings, and failures that cannot separate us from the love of Christ. Romans 8:35 (NIV) states, "Who shall separate us from the love of Christ? *Shall* tribulation, or distress, or persecution, or famine, or nakedness, or peril, or sword?" In essence, the word of God is encouraging us not to quit. *Quitting* is a word that has a lot of force. Sometimes a process is so challenging that the temptation to quit is real. Many people quit because they did not get an expedient result. Their expectations were not met. They were let down. In fact, many of life's challenges or transitions are not expected. However, those who have a method of dealing with their issues, facing the challenges, and a willingness to confront adversity have a higher probability of overcoming "in all these things." More importantly, God's word assures us that we are more than conquerors "through [Him] who loved us" (Romans 8:37, NIV). Jesus experienced temptations, betrayal, rejection, and suffering to show us how to endure. Because Christ lives in us, He gives us the power to be "more than conquerors."

Don't quit! Christ loves us too much. Don't quit because we don't see any changes yet. The changes will come in His timing. Once we accept the situation or claim a victim mentality, we empower the circumstances to dominate us. Our emotions may be leading us instead of us leading it. Don't quit on ourselves! We have a creator who loves us and created us in His image and likeness. Therefore, we are important to Him. How we see ourselves determines how we see our opportunities, challenges, issues, the people around us, and our future.

Declaration of Faith
God, help us not to quit on ourselves but help us to see that we are more than conquerors because you loved us and died for us. Therefore, we have purpose, and we must reach our destinies in you. This is my declaration in the name of Jesus.

Day 5: Reflection
Don't Quit

Romans 8:37 (NIV): "No, in all these things we are more than conquerors through [Him] who loved us."

1. Reflect on the key words in the passage that are most relevant to you.
2. Reflect on a time that you quit or wanted to quit. What lessons did you learn?
3. What are two Bible verses that come to mind after reading this passage?
4. What are your thoughts on this particular passage, and how do you think your thoughts and behavior will improve in the future?

NOTES

DAY 6

GOD'S KNOWLEDGE AND *Purpose*

Romans 8:28 (NKJV)

DAY 6

God's Knowledge and Purpose

Romans 8:28 (NKJV): "And we know that all things work together for good to those who love God, to those who are the called according to *His* purpose."

I recall a very stimulating discussion in one of my final classes at Rutgers University before graduation. The professor was asking questions about knowing, knowledge, and wisdom. With confidence, I thought, I am pretty knowledgeable. As if the professor read my thoughts, he put me on the spot and asked, "Are you more knowledgeable than a grandmother of five?" I thought, oh definitely! Then the professor went on to fill in more details. The grandmother has lived longer than you. She has had many more life experiences. She has survived many more situations and has met many more people. She has been places that you haven't been. You may be more book smart, but you have not had as many experiences as the grandmother of five. Life is more than just being book smart. One of the ways to gain knowledge is through life experiences. Now, compared to the grandmother of five, how much more knowledgeable is the Sovereign Lord? He knows all things. He alone can make sense out of the complications in life. We are encouraged to seek God and to know His will and purpose for all aspects of our lives. In knowing, we should demonstrate confidence. We should be well assured. Right? Not always! Even when we know, we sometimes have doubts. Doubts hinder the best of us from walking in God's favor. God assures us that even when we don't know or don't understand the situation, He makes "all things work together for good" (Romans 8:28, NKJV). Is it so that we can get the credit? Of course not! God will work circumstances for our good to get the glory out of the situation. Most times, we don't even know what to say in our prayers. But God in His sovereignty speaks on our behalf. God can see what we don't see. Even when we think we know, it is best to let the Lord who knows all things have the final say in the matter. Why? God has too much invested in us. God called each of His children to accomplish His purpose. God's ultimate purpose is for others to know about the death, burial, resurrection, and return of Jesus through us as we share and illustrate by example the word of God. Do you know God's purpose for your life? Or for your family? Or for your church? Or for your business? Or for your career? Be confident that God will work all things out for your good.

Declaration of Faith
Lord, help me to know without a doubt that you have all things under control. Lord, remind me that you have too much invested in me and that you'll do what is best for me even when I don't understand it at the moment. This is my declaration in the name of Jesus.

Day 6: Reflection
God's Knowledge and Purpose

Romans 8:28 (NKJV): "And we know that all things work together for good to those who love God, to those who are the called according to *His* purpose."

1. Reflect on the key words in the passage that are most relevant to you.
2. Do you think God's knowledge and purpose are relevant?
3. What are two Bible verses that come to mind after reading this passage?
4. What are your thoughts on this particular passage, and how do you think your thoughts and behavior will improve in the future?

NOTES

DAY 7

SHIELD OF *Faith*

EPHESIANS 6:16 (NKJV)

DAY 7
Shield of Faith

Ephesians 6:16 (NKJV): "Above all, taking the shield of faith with which you will be able to quench all the fiery darts of the wicked one."

The purpose of a shield is to protect, to serve as a barrier against attacks, and to keep away potential harm from invading our personal space or destroying the mind and body. Christians take the shield of faith as armor in spiritual battle. "Above all, taking the shield of faith" (Eph. 6:16, NKJV). In daily life we need: the shield of faith to go on when all else fails, the faith to stay focused on the promises of God, and the faith to believe that God will never leave us or forsake us. Life's challenges can be intense (e.g., unemployment, addictions, chronic disability, and divorce). In these challenges, many of us may experience wavering faith. The wicked one (Satan) will try his best to dominate our minds with constant worry and stress, to make us focus on the negative, and to make us believe that God has forgotten us. It is on this mental battlefield that we take the shield of faith. As good soldiers, we should activate our shield to counteract the adversary's weapons. When he launches doubts and assaults of worry, we counteract him by deciding not to dwell on the negative thoughts that come to our mind. Satan is crafty. After you receive a worrisome call from a friend, he will replay the anxieties and what ifs over and over in your mind. But we don't have to be a prisoner to his assaults. Stop the tape from playing on repeat. Use the shield of faith, which is a defensive weapon to block Satan's attacks. Then take the offense, and grab your sword which is the word of God. Launch the promises of God back at him to defeat him. The truth of God's word cancels doubt. How can we strengthen our faith shield? The Bible tells us that faith is built through hearing, reading, studying, and applying the word of God. Think back on each time God delivered you. These are past victories that have been won. This is your trophy case to remind you that the shield of faith works. As a result, we will be prepared to face future challenges.

Declaration of Faith
Lord, help me take up the shield of faith. With my shield of faith, I will counteract and extinguish all the flaming arrows of the evil one. This is my declaration in the name of Jesus.

Day 7: Reflection
Shield of Faith

Ephesians 6:16 (NKJV): "Above all, taking the shield of faith with which you will be able to quench all the fiery darts of the wicked one."

1. Reflect on the key words in the passage that are most relevant to you.
2. What is the shield of faith? How can you strengthen your shield of faith?
3. What are two Bible verses that come to mind after reading this passage?
4. What are your thoughts on this particular passage, and how do you think your thoughts and behavior will improve in the future?

NOTES

DAY 8

Distractions

〙

2 Samuel 11:1-2 (NKJV): "It happened in the spring of the year, at the time when kings go out *to battle*, that David sent Joab and his servants with him, and all Israel; and they destroyed the people of Ammon and besieged Rabbah. But David remained at Jerusalem. Then it happened one evening that David arose from his bed and walked on the roof of the king's house. And from the roof he saw a woman bathing, and the woman *was* very beautiful to behold."

David was a mighty warrior tested as a shepherd against a lion, bear, and Goliath. He was a man after God's own heart, a worshiper, and a man with a purpose. These kingly attributes did not prevent him from being distracted. Just one moment of distraction can lead to regrets, remorse, shattered dreams, and a ruined reputation. In David's case, one stray gaze on the rooftop (a fleeting distraction) led to adulterous desire. He willfully chose to fulfill that desire and committed adultery with Bathsheba, Uriah's wife. When David found out that Bathsheba was pregnant with his baby, David had Uriah killed. That one distracted look led David to a chain reaction of painful consequences. Distractions may come at the wrong time and deter us from doing what's right. It takes discipline, focus, and understanding to combat distraction. God's word reminds us that we have to be vigilant. If not, we may find ourselves unintentionally distracted. As believers, God gives us the Holy Spirit as a guide. When the Holy Spirit speaks to us, we should be sensitive to His guidance. We can train ourselves to develop the habits of listening to the voice of the Holy

Spirit. The thoughts we rehearse in our minds have the highest potential to manifest into actions. We are encouraged to identify our distractions and systematically learn how to resist distractions and stay focused.

Declaration of Faith

Lord, please help me to stay focused on the tasks you have for me. Lord, strengthen me, and give me discernment to decipher what is best in every situation. This is my declaration in the name of Jesus.

Day 8: Reflection Distractions

2 Samuel 11:1-2 (NKJV): "It happened in the spring of the year, at the time when kings go out *to battle*, that David sent Joab and his servants with him, and all Israel; and they destroyed the people of Ammon and besieged Rabbah. But David remained at Jerusalem. Then it happened one evening that David arose from his bed and walked on the roof of the king's house. And from the roof he saw a woman bathing, and the woman *was* very beautiful to behold."

1. Reflect on the key words in the passage that are most relevant to you.
2. If you were distracted, what would you do differently to overcome and stay focused on a godly path?
3. What are two Bible verses that come to mind after reading this passage?
4. What are your thoughts on this particular passage, and how do you think your thoughts and behavior will improve in the future?

NOTES

DAY 9
PREGNANCY AND *Anticipation*

Luke 1:39–41 (NIV)

DAY 9

Pregnancy and Anticipation

Luke 1:39-41 (NIV): "At that time Mary got ready and hurried to a town in the hill country of Judea, where she entered Zechariah's home and greeted Elizabeth. When Elizabeth heard Mary's greeting, the baby leaped in her womb, and Elizabeth was filled with the Holy Spirit."

Pregnancy is a time of anticipation, preparation, and uncertainty. It can be a time of great joy. When my wife was pregnant with our son, James Du Bois Raphael, I was very excited and humbled during the process. One evening, I recalled touching my wife's belly. When I felt my son moving for the first time, the experience took me to another dimension. I felt connected to him without seeing his face. I felt like providing for him everything that he would ever need. I looked forward to teaching him about life and Christian values. I was confident that my son was with us even though we couldn't see him or hold him. We were already a family. We were already connected. In this same way, God has a spiritual connection with each of us. Even when we don't see him or feel him, He is right there. Imagine that the Messiah's presence in Mary's womb has set the atmosphere for expectation and divine connection. Therefore, when Mary greeted Elizabeth, the baby in Elizabeth's womb leaped, and Elizabeth was filled with the Holy Ghost. God wants to speak to us and fill us with His Spirit. He wants to anoint us for what He has purposed for us. The Holy Spirit, who is the Comforter, has sustained my family in the time of pain, grief, and distress. Before we were engaged, my wife's doctor explained that based on several ultrasound results she would not be able to conceive a child naturally. The doctor counseled us to pursue our options through fertility specialists. After we were married, we were elated to learn that my wife was pregnant. In the first trimester, we found out that she was carrying twins and we were overjoyed! That was a double miracle. Soon after, sadly we received the news that one baby had passed away. We were devastated. The Lord kept us through this journey by allowing many persons to speak words of life to us. Many people were praying for us. Our support system was strong, and God brought us through. Six months after those difficult days, our son James Du Bois was born. God preserved our anticipation to be parents, and He gave us a miracle son.

Declaration of Faith
Lord, thank you for my family. We anticipate great things. We are grateful for your grace, mercy, and Holy Spirit. This is my declaration in the name of Jesus.

Day 9: Reflection
Pregnancy and Anticipation

Luke 1:39-41 (NIV): "At that time Mary got ready and hurried to a town in the hill country of Judea, where she entered Zechariah's home and greeted Elizabeth. When Elizabeth heard Mary's greeting, the baby leaped in her womb, and Elizabeth was filled with the Holy Spirit."

1. Reflect on the key words in the passage that are most relevant to you.
2. Reflect on being pregnant with purpose, and reflect on anticipating your dreams to come true.
3. What are two Bible verses that come to mind after reading this passage?
4. What are your thoughts on this particular passage, and how do you think your thoughts and behavior will improve in the future?

NOTES

DAY 10

FOCUS ON *God*

2 Timothy 1:7 (NLT)

James Raphael Enterprises
Inspiring the Leadership Potential in You

DAY 10

Focus on God

2 **Timothy 1:7 (NLT)**: "For God has not given us a spirit of fear and timidity, but of power, love and self-discipline."

Focus is refining the view of a lens until the view is crystal clear. Focusing on God is refining how we see and understand Him in light of His word. To reach our God-given destiny, we need power, love, and self-discipline. The words *power* and *love* are very attractive. They reveal status and importance. However, the word *discipline* in some aspects is not an attractive word. Discipline denotes work, effort, determination, and willingness to stay the course. In second Timothy 1:7, Paul is encouraging Timothy to stay faithful and focused on doing the work of God. In doing God's work, we'll find opposition, disappointments, and joy at the same time. Therefore, it is paramount to have a disciplined life. In other words, practicing a disciplined life gives us the courage to stay focused on what is important. Discipline is adhering to the Christian values that our parents, mentors, and spiritual leaders have taught and instilled in our lives. In living a disciplined life according to the teachings of the Bible, Paul is reminding Timothy of the faith of his mother and grandmother. Focusing on God requires faith. Furthermore, Paul is challenging Timothy to put his faith into practice. Paul reminds him that fear will try to deter him from seeing what God has in store for him. More importantly, fear will keep him from using his gift. Fear will paralyze and prevent him from reaching his full God-given potential. The takeaway message here is that there will be opposition to our dreams, vision, purpose, and destiny. The question is how will we respond? We must know one thing: "God has not given us a spirit of fear and timidity, but of power, love and self-discipline" (2 Timothy 1:7, NLT). God gave us power, love and self-discipline to impact the kingdom of God and the world positively for Christ.

Declaration of Faith

Father God, in the name of Jesus, I ask that you give me the desire to focus on you and to maintain a disciplined life. Lord, as you increase in my life, allow me to be fearless and to have more power in you, more love, and more self-discipline in all aspects of my life. This is my declaration in the name of Jesus!

Day 10: Reflection
Focus on God

2 Timothy 1:7 (NLT): "For God has not given us a spirit of fear and timidity, but of power, love and self-discipline."

1. Reflect on the key words in the passage that are most relevant to you.
2. Reflect on how to remain focus on God in the good and uncertain times.
3. What are two Bible verses that come to mind after reading this passage?
4. What are your thoughts on this particular passage, and how do you think your thoughts and behavior will improve in the future?

James Raphael

NOTES

DAY 11

Vision

Mark 8:22-25 (NKJV)

James Raphael Enterprises
Inspiring the Leadership Potential in You

DAY 11

Vision

◊

Mark 8:22-25 (NKJV): Then He came to Bethsaida; and they brought a blind man to Him, and begged Him to touch him. So He took the blind man by the hand and led him out of the town. And when He had spit on his eyes and put His hands on him, He asked him if he saw anything. And he looked up and said, "I see men like trees, walking." Then He put *His* hands on his eyes again and made him look up. And he was restored and saw everyone clearly.

The gifts of natural and spiritual sight are wonderful, and sometimes many have taken those gifts for granted. Jesus and His disciples went to Bethsaida, and the people brought Jesus a blind man to heal. The people begged Jesus to touch the blind man. It would appear that the people believed that Jesus could heal the blind man. Compared to other healings of blindness, Jesus did something differently. It is important to note that God has the ability to get the desired result in a variety of ways. In verse 23, Jesus "took the blind man by the hand, and led him out of the town." Why would Jesus lead the blind man out of Bethsaida? Bethsaida may have represented a comfort zone for the blind man. Bethsaida may have had a reputation related with unbelief in the things of God. However, the Bible did not specify why Jesus led the blind man out of Bethsaida. I believe Jesus's method of healing the blind man was to disrupt the norm. "When [Jesus] had spit on his eyes, and put [His] hands upon him, [Jesus] asked him if he saw anything" (Mark 8:23, NKJV). In the first stage, the blind man "looked up, and said, I see men like trees, walking" (Mark 8: 24,

NKJV). Then, Jesus "put His hands on his eyes again and made him look up. And he was restored, and saw everyone clearly" (Mark 8:25, NKJV). Jesus restored the natural sight of the man who was once blind. The moral of the story is to trust God's process. Will we give up if we don't realize God's desired vision the first time? Or will we persevere until the desired vision comes to pass?

Declaration of Faith
Lord, I want to see what you see by faith. I have a clear spiritual vision. This is my declaration in the name of Jesus.

Day 11: Reflection
Vision

Mark 8:22-25 (NKJV): Then He came to Bethsaida; and they brought a blind man to Him, and begged Him to touch him. So He took the blind man by the hand and led him out of the town. And when He had spit on his eyes and put His hands on him, He asked him if he saw anything. And he looked up and said, "I see men like trees, walking." Then He put *His* hands on his eyes again and made him look up. And he was restored and saw everyone clearly.

1. Reflect on the key words in the passage that are most relevant to you.
2. Reflect on the importance of spiritual vision.
3. What are two Bible verses that come to mind after reading this passage?
4. What are your thoughts on this particular passage, and how do you think your thoughts and behavior will improve in the future?

NOTES

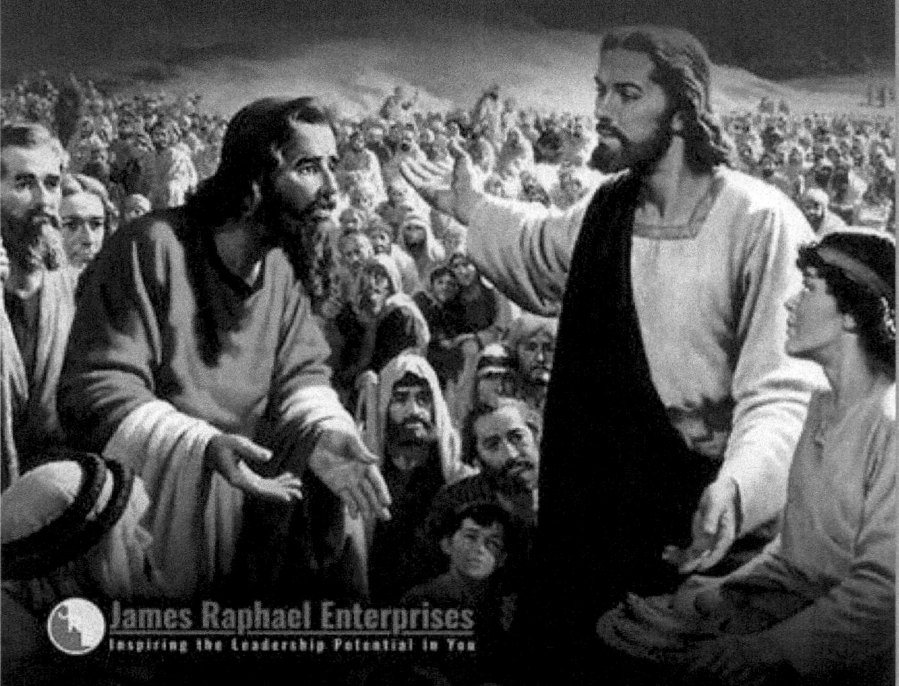

DAY 12

Full Circle

Mark 8:18-19 (NIV): "'Do you have eyes but fail to see, and ears but fail to hear? And don't you remember? When I broke the five loaves for the five thousand, how many basketfuls of pieces did you pick up?' 'Twelve,' they replied."

Reminders are powerful ways to get us to think of what happened, whether positive or negative. The disciples had been with Jesus, and they had seen Him do some great miracles. However, they seemed to forget the great acts Jesus performed. Jesus had to remind His disciples about the feeding of the five thousand: "'When I broke the five loaves for the five thousand, how many basketfuls of pieces did you pick up?' 'Twelve,' they replied" (Mark 8:19, NIV). Frequently, God reminds us that He is still in control. Think back to a situation when you thought the worst was imminent, but in a miraculous way God turned the situation around for you in a positive way. Now, you may find yourself in a new predicament, and you don't know what to do. Jesus is still able to do the miraculous in your life. God is not intimidated by your challenges. In the text, God is reminding us that He provided a way for us before and that He is still able to do the miraculous in our lives. He is the same Jesus. We are reminded that "Jesus Christ is the same yesterday and today and forever" (Hebrews 13:8, NIV). Since Jesus is the same, our trials, tribulations, barriers, and oppositions do not faze Him. Therefore, we are encouraged to rely on His understanding and wisdom. He is with us to guide us through our journey. Even when our eyes fail to see, and ears but fail to hear, God is asking us to trust Him and remember all the good and miraculous things that He has done in our lives and the lives of so many around us. He wants us to understand that coming full circle brings us back to the starting point but with more faith and experience to trust God. We have to take our faith to the next level. The miracles that we've seen with our eyes serve as catalysts to stir up our faith in Jesus and to help us trust Him at His word.

Declaration of Faith

Lord, give me the ability to discern and see with my spiritual eyes and to hear with my spiritual ears. Let me grow beyond my original belief into a deeper conviction of Your divine words and divine ways. This is my declaration in the name of Jesus.

Day 12: Reflection
Full Circle

Mark 8:18-19 (NIV): "'Do you have eyes but fail to see, and ears but fail to hear? And don't you remember? When I broke the five loaves for the five thousand, how many basketfuls of pieces did you pick up?' 'Twelve,' they replied."

1. Reflect on the key words in the passage that are most relevant to you.
2. Reflect on the status of your spiritual eyes and ears.
3. What are two Bible verses that come to mind after reading this passage?
4. What are your thoughts on this particular passage, and how do you think your thoughts and behavior will improve in the future?

NOTES

DAY 13

THE CHURCH

Matthew 4:23 (NIV)

 James Raphael Enterprises
Inspiring the Leadership Potential in You

DAY 13

The Church

§

Matthew 4:23 (NIV): "Jesus went throughout Galilee, teaching in their synagogues, proclaiming the good news of the kingdom, and healing every disease and sickness among the people."

The church can be defined in two ways. First, it is a gathering place for people to worship, praise, and listen to Christ-centered sermons for practical living. Secondly, the church is the body of Christ (people who believe and follow Jesus). Both definitions are true. Just as a company can successfully engage its customer base when it remains true to its brand, as Christians we are most effective when we adhere to our core assignment. Following Jesus's death, burial, and resurrection, He imparted a precise mission to all Christians. Matthew 28:18-20 (NLT) states, "I have been given all authority in heaven and on earth. Therefore, go and make disciples of all the nations, baptizing them in the name of the Father and the Son and the Holy Spirit. Teach these new disciples to obey all the commands I have given you. And be sure of this: I am with you always, even to the end of the age." Like Jesus, we too should witness to our unsaved friends, family members, and neighbors. Differences like race, socioeconomics, education, and reputation are artificial. We are to share the gospel (the good news of the kingdom). Christ died for the sins of humanity. He rose from the dead (a unique occurrence which has not been duplicated). One day, Jesus is coming back for His church and we will be with Him forever (1 Thessalonians 4:13-17, NLT). The gospel has the power to remove obstacles and empower the hearers to be transformed into a new person in

Christ. Through Jesus's example, the church has the great responsibility to make Jesus known throughout the world. In preaching the gospel, the church is able to reach the lost, broken, weary, and hopeless. The church is the light of the world. Just as Jesus went into communities where the people needed Him, and identified with, healed, and ministered to them, remaining distinguished as a vessel of God, so then we should be choice witnesses for the glory of God. In 2004, I traveled as a missionary to Ghana, West Africa, with a team from New Harvest International. The purpose of the mission was to train Ghanaian leaders how to do more effective work for Christ through evangelism and wellness education. It was a joy to visit Accra, Kumasi, and other sites. I met so many Christians devoted to witnessing the gospel of Jesus the Christ to unsaved West Africans in their communities. The people were hungry for the word of God. We had the privilege to share the gospel and many people were blessed.

DECLARATION OF FAITH

The purpose of the church in the world is powerful and essential. We are to evangelize, disciple, and empower people to know that Christ has died, Christ is risen, and Christ will come again. I am committed to fulfilling my essential mission as a Christian. This is my declaration in the name of Jesus.

Day 13: Reflection
The Church

Matthew 4:23 (NIV): "Jesus went throughout Galilee, teaching in their synagogues, proclaiming the good news of the kingdom, and healing every disease and sickness among the people."

1. Reflect on the key words in the passage that are most relevant to you.
2. Reflect on God's purpose for the church.
3. What are two Bible verses that come to mind after reading this passage?
4. What are your thoughts on this particular passage, and how do you think your thoughts and behavior will improve in the future?

James Raphael

NOTES

DAY 14

Authority of Scripture

§

II Peter 1:21 (KJV): "The prophecy came not in old time by the will of man: but holy men of God spake as they were moved by the Holy Ghost."

The Bible is the authoritative word of God. It is immutable. It is infallible. It is eternal. In its sixty-six books, over 33,000 verses were inspired by God to be written by ordinary persons. This God-breathed word is so cohesive that the Old Testament prophets foretold the coming of Jesus centuries before his birth. It was prophesied in Isaiah 7:14 and the prophecy came to pass in Matthew 1:22-23. The authority of scripture did not originate as a human idea, but it germinated in the mind of God. Consider first Thessalonians 2:13 (KJV), "For this reason we also constantly thank God that when you received the word of God which you heard from us, you accepted it not as the word of men, but for what it really is, the word of God, which also performs its work in you who believe." The incontrovertible, heart changing, and soul saving word of God is powerful. Its words are life to the body, spirit, and soul. Accepting the authority of scripture comes through a personal relationship with the author. Hebrews 12:2a says it perfectly: "Looking unto Jesus the author and finisher of *our* faith..." Having faith in the authority of scripture causes it to come alive in your life and mine. The authoritative and living word of God has the power to transform the heart, mind, and life of every reader who aligns with it. The Holy Spirit is a great activator, stirring the faith of every reader and hearer. When we meditate on, and practice what the word of God says, diligently following God's guidance in every aspect of our lives, then we too stand in the authority of God's word. This provides hope, security, and assurance.

Declaration of Faith

Lord, give me the faith that moves mountains and the understanding that your word has authority to break every stronghold and every spirit that is not of God. This is my declaration in the name of Jesus.

Day 14: Reflection
Authority of Scripture

II Peter 1:21 (KJV): "The prophecy came not in old time by the will of man: but holy men of God spake as they were moved by the Holy Ghost."

1. Reflect on the key words in the passage that are most relevant to you.
2. Reflect on how the authority of scripture has kept you strong.
3. What are two Bible verses that come to mind after reading this passage?
4. What are your thoughts on this particular passage, and how do you think your thoughts and behavior will improve in the future?

NOTES

DAY 15

THE WORD OF GOD

2 Timothy 3:16-17 (NIV)

James Raphael Enterprises
Inspiring the Leadership Potential in You

DAY 15

The Word of God

§

2 Timothy 3:16-17 (NIV): "All Scripture is God-breathed and is useful for teaching, rebuking, correcting and training in righteousness, so that the servant of God may be thoroughly equipped for every good work."

Now that we understand the authority of the word of God (Day 14), I assert that God's word empowers us to be effective in life. The purpose of all scripture is to help us understand the mind of God and to empower us to be effective in every good work. But before we become eager beavers to win the world for Christ, we should read the word of God to assess where we are and understand where we should be. With an understanding of scripture, we can allow the word of God to become effective first in us. God's word is a mirror and when we read it, we can see our own nature. We should not get discouraged when we see shortcomings and failure. We are not perfect. However, God's word encourages us to "Study to shew thyself approved unto God, a workman that needeth not to be ashamed, rightly dividing the word of truth" (2 Timothy 2:15, KJV). In studying the word of God, we will understand what God requires of us on a macro-level as Christians, and then on a micro-level, individually. It is this global and local good work that we will be equipped to do God's work efficiently and effectively. Intrinsically, we tend to do what is familiar and pleasing to us. We like to be comfortable, whereas the word of God reveals what needs to change. It corrects, trains, and equips. If you are searching for your purpose, I encourage you to start with the word of God. Let it be your personal GPS. God's word will search you, identifying the coordinates of your current position, and He will direct your path. At each destination, you will be equipped to fulfill your God-given purpose.

Declaration of Faith
Lord, thank you for your word! Continually give me the desire to read, apply, and share your word with everyone. This is my declaration in the name of Jesus.

Day 15: Reflection
The Word of God

2 Timothy 3:16-17 (NIV): "All Scripture is God-breathed and is useful for teaching, rebuking, correcting and training in righteousness, so that the servant of God may be thoroughly equipped for every good work."

1. Reflect on the key words in the passage that are most relevant to you.
2. Reflect on what the word of God means to you.
3. What are two Bible verses that come to mind after reading this passage?
4. What are your thoughts on this particular passage, and how do you think your thoughts and behavior will improve in the future?

NOTES

DAY 16

GOD'S *Plans*

Jeremiah 29:11 (NIV)

DAY 16

God's Plans for Your Life

§

Jeremiah 29:11 (NIV): "'For I know the plans I have for you,' declares the Lord, 'plans to prosper you and not to harm you, plans to give you hope and a future.'"

The people of God spent seventy years in Babylonian captivity as a result of rejecting God. In captivity, they were oppressed and restricted from worshiping God. However, God used His prophet Jeremiah to speak a word of purpose and encouragement to them. Later, God's people would experience His plans of prosperity and hope for their lives. Eventually, God's people returned to Jerusalem and resumed worshipping God Almighty. Jeremiah 29:11 illustrates a truth that is still evident. God has plans for our lives. Even when there is violence, war, and rumors of war in this world, the good news is that God's plans are to prosper us and not to harm us. More importantly, God's plans for us are to give us hope and a future. Who but God can speak to us in such a confident and reassuring way during such turbulent times? The One who knows the end from the beginning and has all power in His hands has given us a glimpse of the future. According to God's track record, we can trust Him at His word. However, it is up to us to search God's word to know His thoughts about us. In knowing God's thoughts, we're more likely to understand His principles, wisdom, instructions, and plans for our lives. God has deposited many gifts within us. I believe that God's word has foundational truths that can help us implement God's plan and become a better person so that our families, friends, colleagues, and others can see a positive difference in us. In searching God's plan for our lives, it is best to stay connected with God through prayer, fasting, praise, worship, and studying God's word. I believe each person must ask several key questions to know and acknowledge God's plans for his or her life. They are the following: Who am I? How is my relationship with God? Why am I here? What am I passionate about? Where am I going? What interests me? What can I do? Here are the steps that I would encourage everyone to follow after answering all the above questions. They are as follows: 1) Write your plan on paper (invite God to intervene as needed). 2) Seek the Lord regarding His plan for your life according to His word. 3) Execute the plan. 4) Evaluate your progress. 5) Get feedback, and adjust your plan as needed. God loves us. He wants the best for us. He tells us his plans. "'For I know the plans I have for you,' declares the LORD, 'plans to prosper you and not to harm you, plans to give you hope and a future'" (Jeremiah 29:11, NIV).

DECLARATION OF FAITH
Lord, I want the plans that you have for my life. I know the plans that you have for me are better than what I have imagined. I am preparing for and expecting great things in my life in the name of Jesus. This is my declaration.

Day 16: Reflection
God's Plans for Your Life

Jeremiah 29:11 (NIV): "'For I know the plans I have for you,' declares the Lord, 'plans to prosper you and not to harm you, plans to give you hope and a future.'"

1. Reflect on the key words in the passage that are most relevant to you.
2. Reflect on God's plans for you and your family.
3. What are two Bible verses that come to mind after reading this passage?
4. What are your thoughts on this particular passage, and how do you think your thoughts and behavior will improve in the future?

NOTES

DAY 17

Salvation

Isaiah 55:8 (KJV)

DAY 17

Salvation

§

Isaiah 55:8 (KJV): "For my thoughts are not your thoughts, neither are your ways my ways, saith the Lord."

How could we ever try to compare our thoughts with God's thoughts? There is no comparison. In the legendary dialogue documented in Job 38, God asks a series of epic questions. In so doing He demonstrates that He is omniscient (all-knowing) and omnipotent (all powerful). "Do you realize the extent of the earth? Tell me about it if you know!"... "Do you know the laws of the universe? Can you use them to regulate the earth?"... "Who gives intuition to the heart and instinct to the mind?" (Job 38:18,33,36, NLT). This larger than life discourse demonstrates the profundity of God's thoughts. He is Alpha (the beginning) and Omega (the end). Acknowledging the frailty of the human mind, Job replied, "I am nothing—how could I ever find the answers? I will cover my mouth with my hand..." (Job 40:4, NLT). Sometimes we think that we are like God, and our prideful actions demonstrate our limited understanding. Unfortunately, when we think that we know the best course of action to pursue, and we move ahead without consulting the Most High, many times we end up with a substandard result. Regardless of how we've fallen short of God's expectations and standards, He is still calling us to acknowledge His thoughts and His ways. God wants us to seek Him and listen to his counsel on every matter. There is a distinction to be made here. Advice comes from a parallel or equal, but only a higher authority can give wise counsel. God wants the best for us. He calls us into His plan, path, and perspective which is new life in Him. The first man, Adam, fell short of God's plan for unity and relationship through sin. Every person that has ever lived has sinned; the very essence of which separates us from God. Even the great characters in the Bible were still human and they sinned. In God's infinite wisdom, through 42 generations from Abraham to Jesus (Matthew 1:17, KJV), God unfolded a plan to save all humanity from sin. "And he saw that there was no man, and wondered that there was no intercessor: therefore his arm brought salvation..." (Isaiah 59:16, KJV). God sent his son Jesus as a sacrifice to pay for the sins of the world. And by His sacrifice, we were redeemed. This is known as God's salvific plan for humanity (1 Timothy 2:4-6, NLT). Salvation is simple. No one can buy it. Jesus already paid the ultimate price making salvation a free gift. If you are not saved, I invite you today to respond to God's call. Accept the gift of salvation today. Confess your sins to God. He is a faithful forgiving Savior (1 John 1:9, KJV). Let us accept forgiveness for our sins and receive eternal life.

Declaration of Faith
Lord, my thoughts are not your thoughts, neither are your ways my ways. I accept your salvation today. This is my declaration in the name of Jesus.

Day 17: Reflection
Salvation

Isaiah 55:8 (KJV): "For my thoughts are not your thoughts, neither are your ways my ways, saith the Lord."

1. Reflect on the key words in the passage that are most relevant to you.
2. Reflect on God's salvation plan for you and humanity.
3. What are two Bible verses that come to mind after reading this passage?
4. What are your thoughts on this particular passage, and how do you think your thoughts and behavior will improve in the future?

NOTES

DAY 18

Faith
IN ACTION

James 2:17 (KJV)

DAY 18
Faith in Action

§

James 2:17 (KJV): "Thus also faith by itself, if it does not have works, is dead."

Faith is a significant word. The essence of our lives as Christians is faith. For we know that "…without faith it is impossible to please [Him]: for he that cometh to God must believe that he is, and that he is a rewarder of them that diligently seek [Him]" (Hebrews 11:6, KJV). So what does the word *faith* really mean? Is it simply having *confidence, commitment,* and *conviction*? Yes, these are aspects of faith, but there's so much more. Faith is being so sure of what you don't see yet, that you believe and act as though it really is there (Hebrews 11:1, KJV). James 2:17, is challenging us not only to have faith, but also to take actions that demonstrate our faith. Faith in action can change history. Dr. Martin Luther King Jr. had a dream that one-day blacks and whites would have the same opportunities. With support from many people, King demonstrated faith and works in pursuing and achieving great progress in the civil rights movement. As believers, our faith has unlimited potential when we put it into action. Active faith is believing, declaring, and demonstrating through our works that we believe God. It is good to say that we believe God. However, there should be proof to validate this declaration. Our neighbors cannot see our hearts, but they can see our actions. How do you respond at work when your supervisor does not honor the promise to promote you? Do you act in a way that demonstrates that you believe that your career is in God's hands? Do you understand that this is a platform to demonstrate active faith in front of a bigger audience of your coworkers? Have you continued to do your best work in an ethical way to give God glory? Our faithfulness and faith-filled actions show that we have faith in the true and living God. Faith is the laboratory in which God does His best work. We become recipients of His sustaining power, protection, provision, deliverance, healing, and much more.

Declaration of Faith
Lord, help me to increase my faith in you so that others may know that you are God Almighty! This is my declaration in the name of Jesus.

Day 18: Reflection
Faith in Action

James 2:17 (KJV): "Thus also faith by itself, if it does not have works, is dead."

1. Reflect on the key words in the passage that are most relevant to you.
2. Reflect on how you put your faith in action and were amazed at the result.
3. What are two Bible verses that come to mind after reading this passage?
4. What are your thoughts on this particular passage, and how do you think your thoughts and behavior will improve in the future?

NOTES

DAY 19

Faith THROUGH WORKS

JAMES 2:21 (KJV)

James Raphael Enterprises
Inspiring the Leadership Potential in You

DAY 19
Faith through Works

※

James 2:21 (KJV): "Was not Abraham our father justified by works, when he had offered Isaac his son upon the altar?"

Abraham's conviction led him to take action. Abraham's action demonstrated that he believed God. Actions of faith speak louder than words. These actions are fueled by an unshakable belief system that declares seriousness about what is being displayed. Abraham's offering of Isaac upon the altar is the type of the ultimate sacrifice of Jesus on the cross, offering Himself as the one and only redeemer of humanity. God did not allow Isaac to be killed in the sacrifice. In fact, God provided a ram as a substitute. Genesis 22:13 (NIV) states, "Abraham looked up and there in a thicket he saw a ram caught by its horns. He went over and took the ram and sacrificed it as a burnt offering instead of his son." The word of God encourages believers to be steadfast in their faith. Our faith on display may attract many people who do not know Jesus and give others the perfect opportunity to know more about Him and to commit their lives to the Savior of the world. By developing our faith, unbelievers will see a godly difference in us. When we display Christlike characteristics, we are publicly displaying and confirming the power of the presence of Jesus in our lives. Humanity cannot work its way into heaven by just doing good works. However, God requires those who know Him to take the responsibility to show their faith through their works because they have the heart of Christ. Since we are commissioned to do the work of the Lord (that is to act), we should seek opportunities to demonstrate faith through works to display the power of God in our lives.

Declarations of Faith
Lord, give me the conviction, the strength, the wisdom, the discernment, and the courage to show my faith through my works. This is my declaration in the name of Jesus.

Day 19: Reflection
Faith through Works

James 2:21 (KJV): "Was not Abraham our father justified by works, when he had offered Isaac his son upon the altar?"

1. Reflect on the key words in the passage that are most relevant to you.
2. Reflect on faith and works. Can works save you?
3. What are two Bible verses that come to mind after reading this passage?
4. What are your thoughts on this particular passage, and how do you think your thoughts and behavior will improve in the future?

NOTES

DAY 20
Friend OF GOD
JAMES 2:23 (KJV)

DAY 20

Friend of God

James 2:23 (KJV): "And the scripture was fulfilled which saith, Abraham believed God, and it was imputed unto him for righteousness: and he was called the Friend of God."

How do you define a friend? What are the characteristics of your closest friends that you love the most? How do they add to your life? A friend is someone who looks out for you. A friend wants the best for you. A friend loves you when you are at your best or even your worst. God will always be our truest and most faithful friend. God calls those who believe in Him, have a relationship with Him, and obey Him, a friend. In James 2:23, God called Abraham friend because Abraham put his faith in God into action. Abraham believed God at His word, and he obeyed God's instructions to offer his only son, Isaac as a sacrifice. Abraham's action moved the very heart of God. As a result, God counted Abraham as righteous. Abraham's work alone did not qualify him to be called righteous. However, Abraham's belief in God was the requirement God desired. Based on Abraham's belief in God, God called Abraham His friend and righteous man (or man in right relationship with God). This principle does not only apply to Abraham but to anyone who believes in God. Once we believe in God and commit to His ways, we become His friend. If you know that God is your friend, then you know that no matter what comes your way God is standing right by your side. You can face the challenges. You have the victory.

Declaration of Faith

Lord, your friendship is everlasting. Having you as my friend is the best assurance that I could ever need. This is my declaration in the name of Jesus.

Day 20: Reflection
Friend of God

James 2:23 (KJV): "And the scripture was fulfilled which saith, Abraham believed God, and it was imputed unto him for righteousness: and he was called the Friend of God."

1. Reflect on the key words in the passage that are most relevant to you.
2. Reflect on whether or not God would call you a friend? Would you call God a friend? What is required for God to call you a friend?
3. What are two Bible verses that come to mind after reading this passage?
4. What are your thoughts on this particular passage, and how do you think your thoughts and behavior will improve in the future?

NOTES

DAY 21

Christ
Prince of Peace   Son of Man
                    Chosen One
Lord   Rabbi
                    Son of God
The Way   I AM   Advocate
        The Door   Lamb of God

Prophet

JESUS
John 1:1

God

The Word

King of Kings
                Healer
Alpha and Omega   Jehovah
              Savior

Deliverer   Great High Priest

        Emmanuel
                    Son of David
Mediator
        Light of The World   Messiah

DAY 21
Jesus

John 1:1 (KJV): "In the beginning was the Word, and the Word was with God, and the Word was God."

General revelation is a term used to describe knowing God through nature (e.g., the universe, the animals, plants, and things that He created). Special revelation describes how God revealed Himself to us through Jesus, the primary proof of God's existence. Before time, Jesus existed in eternity past. In John 1:1, we see the full spectrum of who Jesus is and His mission on earth in only one verse. Jesus is God! Jesus is the Word of God! John 1:14 states, "The Word became flesh and made his dwelling among us. We have seen his glory, the glory of the one and only Son, who came from the Father, full of grace and truth" (NIV). The purpose of Jesus's mission on earth was to identify Himself as God and give everyone an opportunity to obtain eternal life. There will come a time when everyone (living and dead) will recognize that Jesus is God. "At the name of Jesus every knee should bow, in heaven and on earth and under the earth, and every tongue confess that Jesus Christ is Lord, to the glory of God the Father" (Philippians 2:10-11, NLT). Every saved man, woman, boy, and girl, finds life through Jesus. John 10:10 declares, "The thief comes only to steal and kill and destroy; I came that they may have life, and have *it* abundantly" (NASB). Jesus is the head of the church. "And He is the head of the body, the church, who is the beginning, the firstborn from the dead, that in all things He may have the preeminence" (Colossians 1:18, NKJV).

Jesus's work and teachings continue to influence the world. "But you will receive power when the Holy Spirit comes upon you. And you will be my witnesses, telling people about me everywhere in Jerusalem, throughout Judea, in Samaria, and to the ends of the earth" (Acts 1:8, NLT). Jesus has established a solid foundation upon Himself. Jesus is the Light of the World, Lord of All, Our Peace, The Truth, Good Shepherd, Our Hope, Chief Cornerstone, and Faithful and True. But He is not limited to these titles. Jesus is God. "For by Him all things were created that are in heaven and that are on earth, visible and invisible, whether thrones or dominions or principalities or powers. All things were created through Him and for Him. And He is before all things, and in Him all things consist" (Colossians 1:16-17, NKJV). Do you know Jesus as your Lord and Savior?

Declaration of Faith

My God, I believe without a doubt, that Jesus is God. I declare that my best days are yet to come and that I will experience abundance in all aspects of my life. I declare that I will live on purpose, for purpose, and impact the world in a positive way. This is my declaration in the name of Jesus!

Prayer for Salvation

Jesus, I ask that you would come into my heart. I repent of my sins. I believe that you are Lord and Savior. I confess with my mouth that you died. I believe in my heart that God raised you from the dead. Those who believe in you should not perish but have everlasting life. I believe in the name of Jesus. I declare that I am saved! Amen!

Day 21: Reflection
Jesus

John 1:1 (KJV): "In the beginning was the Word, and the Word was with God, and the Word was God."

1. Reflect on the key words in the passage that are most relevant to you.
2. Reflect on who is Jesus and what He means to you.
3. What are two Bible verses that come to mind after reading this passage?
4. What are your thoughts on this particular passage, and how do you think your thoughts will improve in the future?

NOTES

ABOUT THE AUTHOR

James Raphael is a licensed nursing home administrator both in New Jersey and New York. He is a certified assisted living administrator (CALA) in New Jersey teaching entrepreneurs and health care professionals how to pass the CALA state test. As a certified Jack Canfield coach, James coaches leaders to become great. James earned his Bachelor of Arts (Rutgers University), Bachelor of Theology (Easter Bible Institute), and Master of Business Administration (University of Phoenix). James is a licensed minister at Cathedral International (Perth Amboy, New Jersey) and has authored his first book, *21 Day Devotional: Declaration of Faith*. Minister Raphael is committed to reaching God's people and humanity through God's word, coaching, leadership success training, and authoring books. Currently, James is an administrator of a community-based program where he led his team to a deficiency-free survey from New Jersey Department of Health. James is the CEO of James Raphael Enterprises (JRE). The mission of JRE is to inspire, empower, and equip individuals and organizations to reach their full potential and make a positive difference in the world. James lives with his wife, Monaé, and son, James Du Bois, in New Jersey.

James Raphael, LNHA, CALA, MBA, and CEO of JRE
http://www.jamesraphael.com

BOOK DESCRIPTION

21 Day Devotional: Declaration of Faith

The purpose of the *21 Day Devotional: Declaration of Faith* is to help readers to:

1. Reflect on the awesomeness of God
2. Remember that God is still in control
3. Receive, apply, and share the authority of scripture
4. Remain focused on the Creator
5. Remember God's plan for their lives and humanity
6. Recall that faith is essential to please God
7. Recognize that Jesus is God

PROMOTIONAL STATEMENTS

§

"In his first book, *21 Day Devotional: Declaration of Faith*, James Raphael has given us something to think about, something to chew on, and something to build a foundation on. It's encouraging, it's inspiring, and it's comforting. I commend my son in faith for this step of faith. We all need somebody to lean on, and someone to help us up the ladder to success. Minister James Raphael is that person. We support James, and I encourage you all to go get a copy, and let's celebrate this work."
- Bishop Donald Hilliard, Jr., D. Min.
Senior Pastor, Cathedral International
Perth Amboy, New Jersey

"Reading Minister James Raphael's *21 Day Devotional: Declaration of Faith* will help you lift your mind and heart to God. Reflecting on the guidance offered and questions asked might just open your ears to hear the voice of God."
- Joseph F. Duffy MAT, MA, MPA, MNM, LLD,
Retired president of Catholic Charities in the Diocese of Paterson, NJ

"James Raphael has put time and thought into this work and he shares from his personal experience of knowing God, being blessed by God and having faith to trust God as He orders his steps. I was blessed by reading this work and I plan to share it with others. A declaration of Faith is so necessary in a world where many people seem to have forgotten God or

have lost sight on the advantage of having Him in their lives. This Journal made me more aware that I am not alone in my convictions about God and His ability to do anything."
- Odessa McNeill, Th.D.
Academic Dean
Pneuma Life School of Ministry, Rahway, NJ
Eastern Bible Institute, Irvington, NJ

www.ingramcontent.com/pod-product-compliance
Lightning Source LLC
Chambersburg PA
CBHW060802050426
42449CB00008B/1490